SPECIAL OLYMPICS

GLOBAL CITIZENS: SPORTS

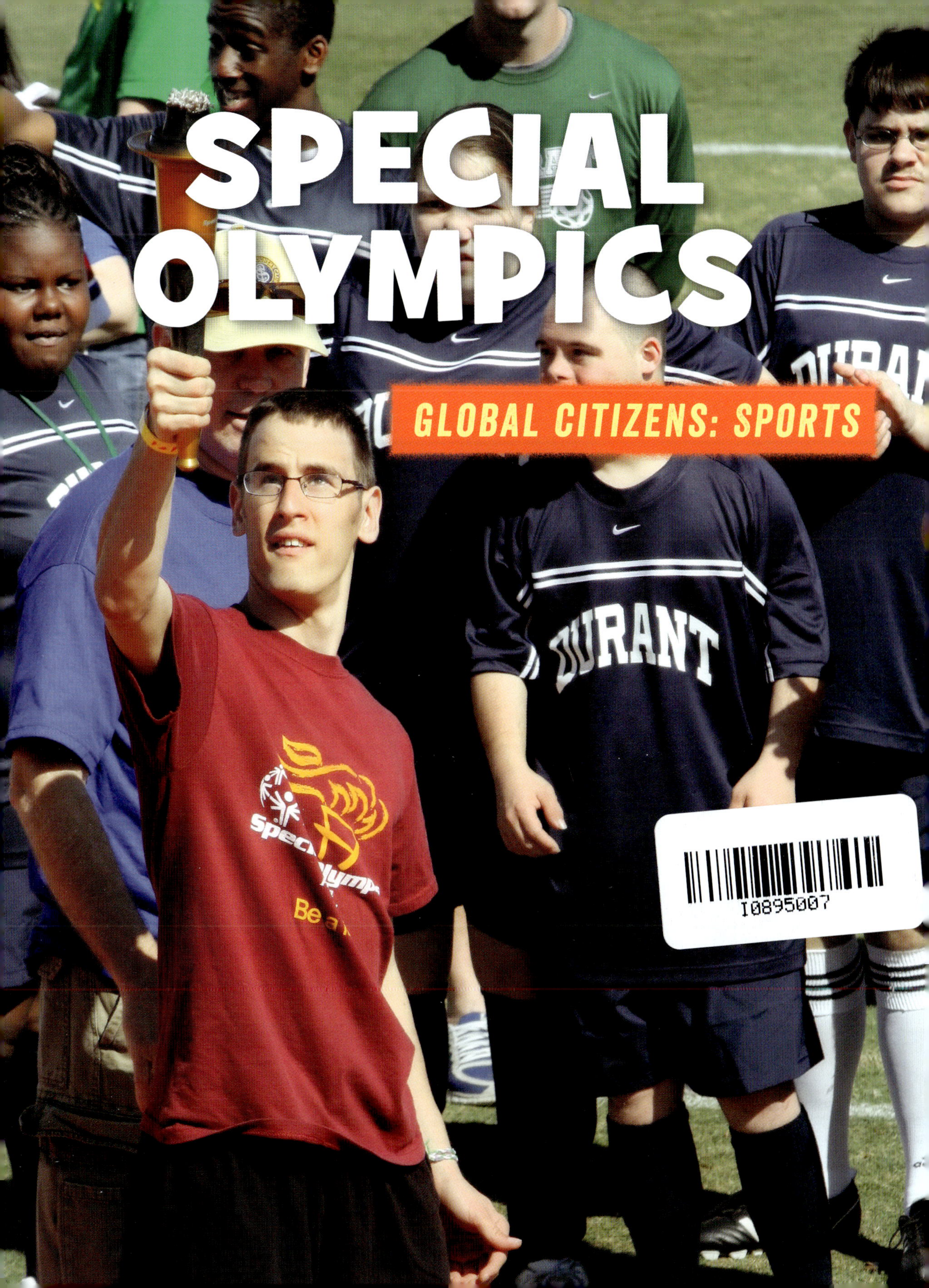

I0895007

Published in the United States of America by Cherry Lake Publishing
Ann Arbor, Michigan
www.cherrylakepublishing.com

Content Adviser: Liv Williams, Editor, www.iLivExtreme.com
Reading Adviser: Marla Conn, MS, Ed., Literacy specialist, Read-Ability, Inc.

Photo Credits: ©dpa picture alliance/Alamy Stock Photo, cover, 5; ©Alexa Sklar/Dreamstime, 1; ©Joseph Sohm/Shutterstock, 7, 8, 14, 28; ©Mahmoud Ghazal/11; ©Tokarsky/Dreamstime, 12; ©Stanislaw Tokarski/Shutterstock, 13, 19; © Kpikoulas/Dreamstime, 17; ©Rose Archives of the College at Brockport, 18; ©hxdbzxy/Shutterstock, 20; ©Jeff Greenberg /age footstock, 22; ©Tamara Lee Harding/Dreamstime, 25; ©Popartic/Shutterstock, 26

Copyright ©2020 by Cherry Lake Publishing
All rights reserved. No part of this book may be reproduced or utilized in any form or by any means without written permission from the publisher.

Library of Congress Cataloging-in-Publication Data

Names: Hellebuyck, Adam, author. | Deimel, Laura, author.
Title: Special Olympics / written by Adam Hellebuyck and Laura Deimel.
Description: Ann Arbor, Michigan : Cherry Lake Publishing, [2019] | Series: Global Citizens: Sports | Audience: Grades 4 to 6 | Includes bibliographical references and index.
Identifiers: LCCN 2019004215 | ISBN 9781534147546 (hardcover) | ISBN 9781534150409 (paperback) | ISBN 9781534148970 (pdf) | ISBN 9781534151833 (hosted ebook)
Subjects: LCSH: Special Olympics—Juvenile literature.
Classification: LCC GV722.5.S64 H45 2019 | DDC 796.087/4—dc23
LC record available at https://lccn.loc.gov/2019004215

Cherry Lake Publishing would like to acknowledge the work of the Partnership for 21st Century Learning. Please visit *www.p21.org* for more information.

Printed in the United States of America
Corporate Graphics

ABOUT THE AUTHORS

Laura Deimel is a fourth grade teacher and Adam Hellebuyck is a high school social studies teacher at University Liggett School in Grosse Pointe Woods, Michigan. They have worked together for the past 8 years and are thrilled they could combine two of their passions, reading and sports, into this work.

TABLE OF CONTENTS

History: Thank Shriver!

The Special Olympics started when Eunice Kennedy Shriver saw that people with **intellectual** disabilities were not given the same opportunities as other people. People with intellectual disabilities might learn new skills more slowly. They might need a little extra help in life. But Shriver saw what many others didn't: people with intellectual disabilities still had their own special talents.

Who Was Eunice Kennedy Shriver?

Shriver was the sister of President John F. Kennedy. Their sister, Rosemary, was born with an intellectual disability. Shriver wanted to do something for people like her sister. In 1962, she was inspired to host a summer camp at her home for young people

About 50 volunteers helped make the 1962 summer camp a wonderful experience.

with disabilities. She called it Camp Shriver. She wanted to prove that people like her sister were just as talented as others, only in a different way.

Shriver and experts discovered that exercise and activity were actually helpful for people with disabilities. This discovery motivated Shriver to create an event that encouraged them to show off their talents.

The First Special Olympics Games

On July 20, 1968, the first Special Olympics were held in Chicago, Illinois. It was called the World Games. The Games quickly became popular and began being held **biennially**. Only U.S. athletes participated in the first Special Olympics, which was called World Games. At this time, the word "Olympics" wasn't allowed to be used in the name yet. After that, other countries started participating.

Using the Word *Olympics*

In 1971, the United States Olympic Committee gave the World Games the right to use the word Olympics *in their competitions. The 1972 games were the first to be called the Special Olympics. There are only four global groups that can be called Olympics: the Olympic Games, the Paralympic Games, the Junior Olympics, and the Special Olympics.*

Every participating Special Olympics athlete, including those in last place, are presented with a ribbon.

There are more than 1 million coaches and volunteers who dedicate their time to the Special Olympics.

In 1977, the first Winter Special Olympics competition was held. The event included sports like skating and skiing. In 1988, the group started the Unified Games program. It combined athletes with and without intellectual disabilities and put them on the same sports team. In 1993, the Special Olympics was held outside of the United States for the first time, in Salzburg, Austria.

Developing Questions

Special Olympic athletes have an **oath** *that they recite at the games: "Let me win. But if I cannot win, let me be brave in the attempt." This oath drives their participation in each event. When you are doing something that is important to you, what do you think about? What makes you do it? What helps you to succeed? If you had to write your own oath, what would you include? Is it more important for you to win or to be brave?*

Geography: Around the World

The international Special Olympics World Games is held every 2 years, but not every athlete can compete in them. After all, there are over 5 million athletes worldwide who participate in Special Olympics events each year. These events are held in local communities, states, and 170 different countries throughout the year. That means different events might be happening at the same time in different places.

Special Olympics Around the United States

The United States has dozens of different Special Olympics organizations. For example, New York has nine different groups

In 2019, the Special Olympics World Games will be held for the first time in the Middle East. It will be in Abu Dhabi in the United Arab Emirates.

that organize events for athletes. These events happen during the summer, fall, and winter. In the summer, events include bowling, powerlifting, and tennis. In the fall, athletes roller-skate, play bocce ball, and golf. In the winter, athletes snowshoe, snowboard, and play floor hockey, along with other winter-related sports.

Arizona has six different groups organizing events. They compete in flag football, badminton, and cheerleading, among other sports. Unlike many other states, Arizona can hold sports events throughout the year thanks to its mild **climate**.

There are almost 5 million athletes who participate in the Special Olympics around the world.

France

Countries around the world also have local Special Olympics organizations. France has 14 different groups organizing events around the country. Many organizations hold soccer games for athletes in France. Local organizations even hold competitions in martial arts, table tennis, and handball.

Over 85 percent of athletes that participate in the Special Olympics are outside of North America.

As of 2017, there are 225 national and state Special Olympic programs in 174 countries.

China

China has over 1 million registered Special Olympics athletes who participate in 34 different sports, including beach volleyball, cricket, and sailing. In 2015, there were 6,660 local competitions for Chinese athletes to participate in. China sent 91 athletes to the 2015 Special Olympics World Games in Los Angeles, California.

Chile

This South American country has over 22,000 athletes who compete in 120 different local events throughout the year. Chilean Special Olympics athletes compete in 12 official sports, such as gymnastics, basketball, and swimming. Chile sent 15 athletes to the 2015 Special Olympics World Games.

Gathering and Evaluating Sources

There are Special Olympics events happening almost every day around the world. Try to find an event organized by the Special Olympics that is happening near you. You can do that by contacting the group that organizes the Special Olympics in your state or country. You can find that information at https://www.specialolympics.org/programs. What events does that group hold for its athletes? What help do they need in order to make the Special Olympics a success? Gather information from past events and think of other ways you may be able to help the program succeed.

Civics: Helping Out

Many volunteers are needed to make the Special Olympics a success for the athletes involved. At the 2019 Special Olympics World Games in the Middle East, almost 7,000 athletes participated with the help of over 20,000 volunteers! There are many ways to volunteer with the Special Olympics, both at the World Games and at local events around you. Volunteer opportunities can be either long-term or short-term.

In 2017, the Special Olympics saw a 6 percent increase in volunteers in North America alone.

The logo is based on a sculpture by Zurab Tsereteli called "Joy and Happiness to All the Children of the World."

Working with Teams and Sports

One example of a long-term Special Olympics volunteer opportunity is coaching a sport or a team. Coaches help athletes learn how to play a sport they are interested in. Coaches also help build players' self-confidence and love of the sport. Another way to volunteer long-term is to serve as a referee or judge for an event. Referees and judges are carefully trained to make sure that the competitions are fair and that all athletes are able to contribute to the best of their ability.

As of 2017, there were almost 30,000 volunteers in Africa!

The Special Olympics also hires people with intellectual disabilities. In 2017, the organization had 204 paid staff with intellectual disabilities!

Helping Out at a Special Olympics Event

There are many tasks that need to happen the day of a Special Olympics event to help make it a success. Some of these short-term volunteer opportunities include timing an event, keeping score, handing out awards to athletes, and helping make sure athletes are ready to compete in each event. Another short-term job is being a photographer. Photographers are responsible for taking pictures of athletes competing in the games, to help inspire the athletes, volunteers, and supporters around the world.

Special Olympics Pledge

The Special Olympics organization created an inclusion **pledge**. *This pledge asks everyone to think about the spirit and goals of the Special Olympics every day. The pledge says:*

> *I pledge to look for the lonely, the isolated, the left out, the challenged and the bullied. I pledge to overcome the fear of difference and replace it with the power of inclusion. I #ChooseToInclude.*

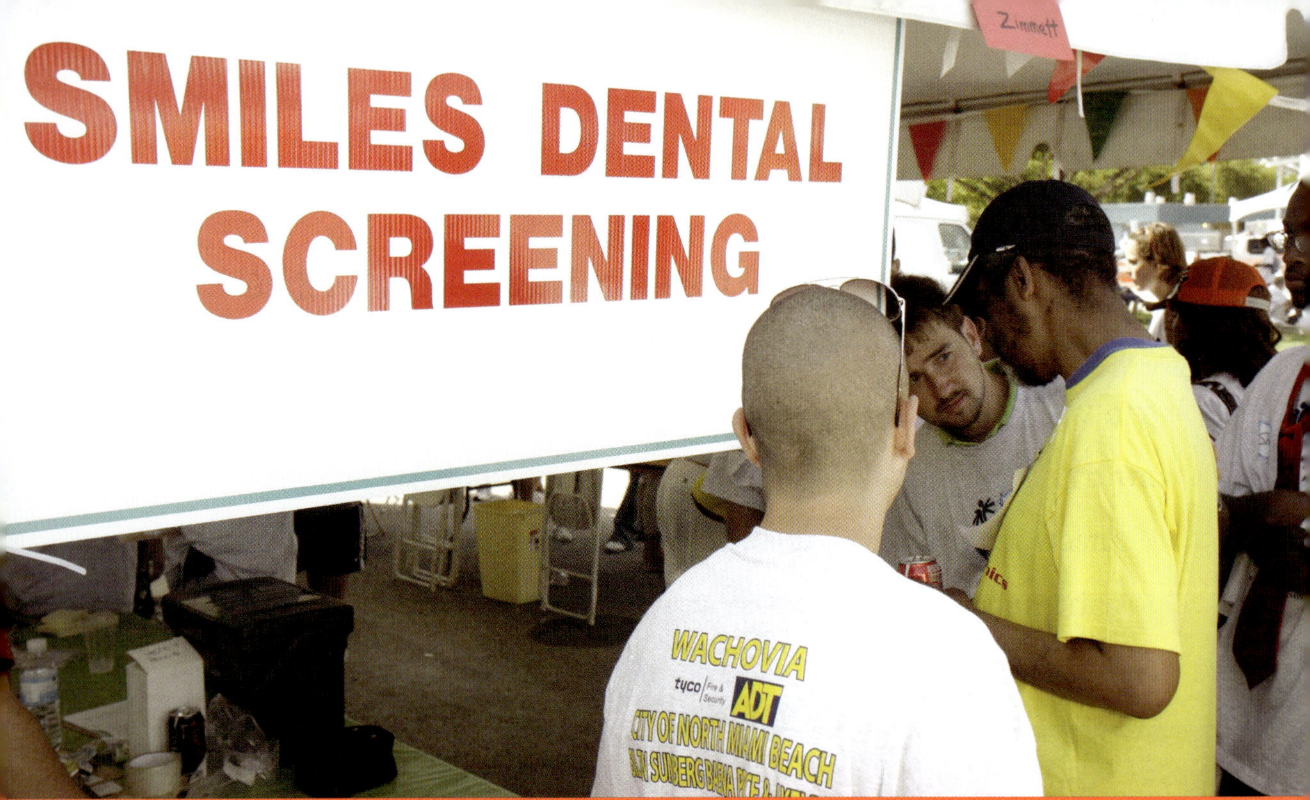

In 2017, the Special Olympics conducted over 195,000 free health screenings.

Without these thousands of volunteers doing many different tasks, Special Olympics events could not happen.

Following the Rules

Volunteers also help the Special Olympics **enforce** their rules for events. Special Olympics athletes have to be at least 8 years old to participate in a sport. Athletes do not have to be an expert in a sport to play. At a Special Olympics event, volunteers organize athletes so they can compete against other people with similar abilities. This ensures all athletes have a chance to do their best.

Encouraging the Athletes

Fans also make the Special Olympics events a success. Cheering on athletes can help encourage them to do their best in the games. It can also let you experience the games and show you what they are all about. You might find that you want to get more involved in the Special Olympics after attending an event as a fan.

Developing Claims and Using Evidence

The Special Olympics created an inclusion pledge to encourage people to stand up for what's right. Do you think pledges make a difference? Why or why not? In what ways do pledges make or not make an impact on an issue? Using your local library and the internet, research this topic further. Use the evidence you find to support your claim. Then, find out how other organizations are using pledges to make a difference in the world.

Economics: Raising Money

The Special Olympics are able to be held because of the many **donations** it gets from thousands of people around the world. The Special Olympics do not charge a fee for athletes to train and compete. This is because the group wants every athlete to be able to compete without having to worry about money.

Money from Foundations

The Special Olympics is a **nonprofit organization**. Any money a nonprofit organization makes is put toward achieving a certain goal. Nonprofits, like the Special Olympics, are open

Many people participate in the polar bear plunge, as pictured, to raise money and awareness for the Special Olympics. This event is held during winter.

The organization offers free health exams to its athletes in 82 countries.

with how they collect and spend their money. This openness encourages more people to work with the organization by donating money or their time and effort.

When the Special Olympics began, the group received most of its money to run the games from the Joseph P. Kennedy Jr. **Foundation**. Today, in order to support over 5 million athletes, the Special Olympics needs to collect money from many different foundations and organizations. In 2015, the Special Olympics received its largest donation—$25 million—from the Golisano Foundation in Los Angeles, California! Even governments can provide the Special Olympics with money so they can run their events. In 2004, the U.S. Congress did this when it passed the Special Olympics Sport and **Empowerment** Act. The act was so popular that every member of Congress voted yes for it.

Taking Informed Action

Now that you know the Special Olympics relies greatly on donations to make the events successful, think about what you could do to raise money for your nearest Special Olympics group. Would you have a bake sale or a lemonade stand? Would you mow lawns, rake leaves, or shovel snow? What is the best way you can think of in your community to raise money for the Special Olympics?

Raising or sending money is not the only way to contribute to the Special Olympics. What other ways could you donate to the Special Olympics?

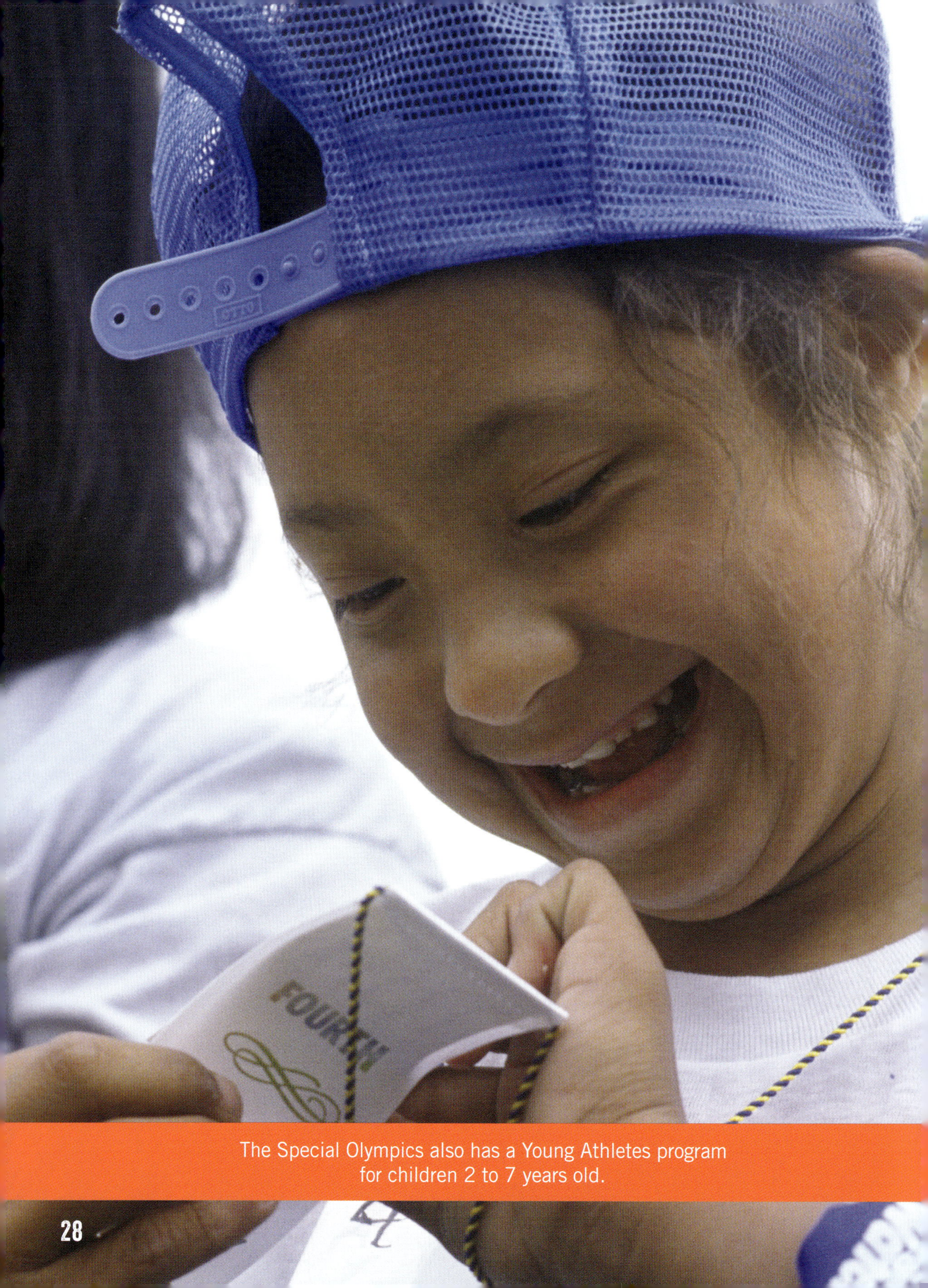

The Special Olympics also has a Young Athletes program for children 2 to 7 years old.

Money from Donations

The Special Olympics also collects donations from thousands of individuals who want to support the group. Some of these donations come from people who have a personal connection to the events. They might have a family member who competed in the games or who has volunteered to help in the past. Other donations come from people who believe in the Special Olympics' goal and want it to succeed.

Communicating Conclusions

Before reading this book, did you know much about the Special Olympics? Now that you know more, why do you think this is an important organization? Do you think more people should donate their time and money to support the Special Olympics? Share what you learned about the organization with friends at school or with your family. Ask them what they think about the Special Olympics.

Think About It

According to a national poll, 34 percent of all people with intellectual disabilities have jobs. But 52 percent of the athletes who participate in the Special Olympics have jobs. Why do you think this is? Do you think that the Special Olympics have an impact on whether people have a job? Besides physical activity, how else can playing a sport help people improve their lives?

Imagine that the Special Olympics did not exist. Do you think that more or fewer people with intellectual disabilities would have jobs? Why do you think that?

For More Information

Further Reading

Kennedy, Mike. *Special Olympics.* New York, NY: Childrens Press, 2003.

Websites

Special Olympics
https://www.specialolympics.org
Visit the official Special Olympics website to discover more about the organization and how you can get involved.

Special Olympics—Young Athletes
https://www.specialolympics.org/our-work/young-athletes
Learn more about how the Special Olympics works with young athletes.

GLOSSARY

biennially (bye-EN-ee-uhl-ee) every two years

climate (KLYE-mit) the types of weather common in a certain area

donations (doh-NAY-shuhnz) things given to a charity to help it achieve its goal

empowerment (em-POU-ur-muhnt) the permission to do something

enforce (en-FORS) to make someone follow a rule

foundation (foun-DAY-shuhn) a group that is dedicated to donating money to other organizations with similar beliefs and goals

intellectual (in-tuh-LEK-choo-uhl) something related to thinking and other mental activities

nonprofit organization (nahn-PRAH-fit or-guh-nih-ZAY-shuhn) a group that wants to achieve a goal other than making money

oath (OHTH) a promise

pledge (PLEJ) a promise or agreement

INDEX